D0803499

Let's Bake
Halloween
Treats!

By Ruth Owen

Gareth Stevens
PUBLISHING

Please visit our website, www.garethstevens.com.
For a free color catalog of all our high-quality books,
call toll free 1-800-542-2595 or fax 1-877-542-2596.

Cataloging-in-Publication Data

Names: Owen, Ruth.
Title: Let's bake Halloween treats! / Ruth Owen.
Description: New York : Gareth Stevens Publishing, 2018. | Series: Holiday baking party | Includes index.
Identifiers: LCCN ISBN 9781538213322 (pbk.) | ISBN 9781538213346 (library bound) | ISBN 9781538213339 (6 pack)
Subjects: LCSH: Halloween cooking--Juvenile literature. | Desserts--Juvenile literature.
Classification: LCC TX739.2.H34 O94 2018 | DDC 641.5'68--dc23

Published in 2018 by
Gareth Stevens Publishing
111 East 14th Street, Suite 349
New York, NY 10003

Produced for Gareth Stevens Publishing by Ruby Tuesday Books Ltd
Designers: Tammy West and Emma Randall

Photo Credits: Courtesy of Ruby Tuesday Books and Shutterstock: P 4 Shutterstock / Veronica Louro;
p 22 Shutterstock / Darren Baker.

Printed in the United States of America

CPSIA compliance information: Batch CS18GS: For further information contact
Gareth Stevens, New York, New York at 1-800-542-2595.

Contents

Let's Get Baking!

The spookiest night of the year is almost upon us. So it's time to get the party started by baking some delicious Halloween treats.

Halloween is always more fun with friends. Invite some friends over for a holiday baking party!

Get Ready to Bake

- Before cooking, always wash your hands well with soap and hot water.
- Make sure the kitchen countertop and all your equipment is clean.
- Read the recipe carefully before you start cooking. If you don't understand a step, ask an adult to help you.
- Gather together all the ingredients and equipment you will need. Baking is more fun when you're prepared!

Measuring cup

Measuring spoons

Measuring Counts

- Make sure you measure your ingredients carefully. If you get a measurement wrong, it could affect how successful your baking is.
  - Use measuring scales or a measuring cup to measure dry and liquid ingredients.
  - Measuring spoons can be used to measure small amounts of ingredients.

Have Fun, Stay Safe!

It's very important to have an adult around whenever you do any of the following tasks in the kitchen:

- Using a mixer, the stovetop burners, or an oven.
- Using sharp utensils, such as knives and vegetable peelers or corers.
- Working with heated pans, pots, or baking sheets. Always use oven mitts when handling heated pans, pots, or baking sheets.

When you've finished baking, ALWAYS clean up the kitchen and put all your equipment away.

Ingredients:

To make the cookie dough:
- 1 ½ cups all-purpose flour (plus a little extra for dusting)
- ½ cup powdered sugar
- 5 ounces butter or margarine (plus a little for greasing)
- 1 orange

To make the filling:
- 3 ½ ounces mascarpone cheese
- 1 teaspoon powdered sugar
- 1 heaping tablespoon semisweet chocolate chips

To make the glaze:
- ½ cup powdered sugar
- 1 tablespoon orange juice

Equipment:
- 2 large cookie sheets
- Mixing bowl
- Wooden spoon
- Grater
- Plastic wrap
- Rolling pin
- 3-inch (8-cm) round cookie cutter
- Small, sharp knife
- Oven mitt
- Heatproof bowl
- Small saucepan
- Small dish
- Brush

Orange Jack-o'-Lantern Cookies

Bake up a batch of scrumptious, orange-flavored jack-o'-lantern cookies to share with your friends after trick-or-treating. The **dough** is fruity, the **glaze** is sticky, and the cookies are filled with a chocolate-cheese frosting.

Step 1 Grease the cookie sheets with a little butter to keep your cookies from sticking to the sheets.

Step 2 Put the butter and sugar into the mixing bowl and **beat** with a wooden spoon until smooth and fluffy.

Step 3 Wash the orange and finely grate its rind to get **zest**. Cut the orange in half and squeeze the juice out in a bowl.

Step 4 Add the flour and orange zest to the bowl and beat the mixture until the ingredients are blended and become crumbly. Next, use your hands to squeeze and **knead** the mixture to make a ball of soft dough.

Step 5 Wrap the dough in plastic wrap and place in a refrigerator for one hour.

Step 6 **Preheat** the oven to 350°F (180°C).

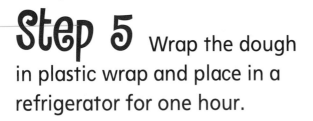

Step 7

Dust your countertop with a little flour. Unwrap the dough and place it on the dusted surface. Roll out the dough to about a quarter of an inch (0.5 cm) thick.

cookie dough

Step 8

Cut 24 circles from the dough and place them on the cookie sheets.

Step 9

On 12 of the circles (the front halves of the cookies) cut the eyes, nose, and mouth of a jack-o'-lantern. Using the blunt edge of your knife, make lines down the faces, too. Shape small pieces of dough into stalks and press them onto the faces.

Front of cookie

Stalk

Back of cookie

The remaining 12 circles will form the back halves of the cookies.

Step 10

Bake the cookies for about 15 minutes, or until they are turning golden. Remove the cookies from the oven using an oven mitt and allow to cool completely.

Step 11
To make the filling, beat the powdered sugar and mascarpone cheese until they are creamy and smooth.

Step 12
Put the chocolate chips into the heatproof bowl. Add about 1 inch (2.5 cm) of water to the saucepan and set the bowl in the saucepan. Heat the saucepan on a medium heat, stirring the chocolate until it melts.

How to melt chocolate

Step 13
Wearing an oven mitt, remove the bowl from the saucepan. Allow the melted chocolate to cool for about 5 minutes. Then add the chocolate to the mascarpone and sugar and mix thoroughly.

The mixture should be a **consistency** similar to peanut butter.

Step 14
To make the glaze, mix the powdered sugar and orange juice until smooth and shiny.

Glaze

Filling

Step 15
Spread some filling onto each of the plain cookie halves. Paint a thin layer of glaze over each face. Allow the glaze to dry, and then squash the two halves of each cookie together. Enjoy!

Ingredients:

To make the cupcake batter:
- 7 ounces butter or margarine
- 1 cup superfine sugar
- 2 cups cake flour
- 1 teaspoon baking powder
- ¼ teaspoon salt
- 3 large eggs
- ½ teaspoon vanilla extract
- ½ cup milk

For the decorations and frosting:
- 3 cups powdered sugar
- 6 tablespoons milk
- Green food coloring
- 36 white mini marshmallows
- Tube of black frosting (with a nozzle for piping)

Equipment

- 12-hole muffin pan
- 12 muffin cases
- Mixing bowl
- Wooden spoon
- Electric mixer (optional)
- Oven mitt
- Potholder
- Metal skewer
- Wire rack for cooling
- Small serrated knife
- Small bowl
- Spoon
- Scissors

Monster Cupcakes

Everyone loves cupcakes, so Halloween is the perfect time to get creative with your cupcake making. These gruesomely green cakes are decorated to look like the face of the slow-moving, groaning monster from the Frankenstein horror movies. Bake up a batch of delicious cupcakes and then get your friends together to carve out the faces and have fun frosting.

Step 1 Preheat the oven to 350°F (180°C).

Step 2 Line the muffin pan with the muffin cases.

Muffin pan

Muffin cases

Electric mixer

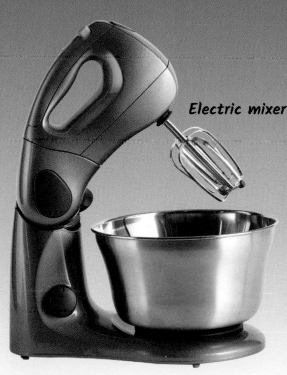

Step 3 Put the butter and sugar into the mixing bowl and **cream together** with a wooden spoon until fluffy. If you wish, you can use an electric mixer for this step.

Step 4 Add the flour, baking powder, salt, eggs, vanilla extract, and milk. Use a wooden spoon or electric mixer to beat the ingredients together until the mixture is thick and smooth.

Cupcake batter

Step 5
Spoon the mixture into the muffin cases, dividing it equally.

Step 6
Bake the cakes for 20 minutes, or until they are golden and have risen above the edges of the muffin cases. To test if the cakes are baked, insert a metal skewer into one cake. If it comes out clean, the cakes are ready.

Step 7
Place the muffin pan on a potholder for about 5 minutes to cool. Then carefully place each cake on the wire rack and allow to cool completely.

Step 8
To carve the monster's face, carefully cut a small semicircle from each side of the cake with a serrated knife.

Forehead

Face

Step 9
Next, slice off any raised part of the cake to create a flat surface. Then cut down into this surface and carve off a thin slice to create the raised forehead and face.

step 10 Mix the powdered sugar, milk, and green food coloring to make the frosting. Add the green coloring in small drops. You can always add more, but you can't remove coloring once it's in the mixture!

The frosting should be smooth and thick, and slowly run off the spoon. If it's too thin or too thick, add more sugar or milk.

step 11 Slowly **drizzle** the frosting over the cakes and allow it to flow over the faces. Add more frosting as needed and help smooth it into place with the spoon.

Put the cakes into the refrigerator for about 15 minutes to help the frosting set.

step 12 Use two marshmallows to be the bolts on the monster's neck. Cut one marshmallow in half to make the white parts of its eyes.

step 13 Use the black frosting to create the monster's hair, eyebrows, pupils, nose, and mouth.

Pumpkin Cupcakes

Ingredients:

To make the cupcake batter:
- 7 ounces butter or margarine
- 1 cup superfine sugar
- 2 cups cake flour
- 1 teaspoon baking powder
- ¼ teaspoon salt
- 3 large eggs
- ½ teaspoon vanilla extract
- ½ cup milk
- Orange food coloring

For the decorations and frosting:
- 1¼ cups powdered sugar
- 1 cup butter (tightly packed)
- 2 tablespoons milk
- Orange and green food coloring
- Mini white marshmallows
- Tube of black frosting

Equipment:

- 6-hole muffin pan
- 6 muffin cases
- Mixing bowl
- Wooden spoon
- Electric mixer (optional)
- Oven mitt
- Potholder
- Metal skewer
- Wire rack for cooling
- 2 small dishes
- 2 spoons
- Small serrated knife
- Icing syringe (optional)
- Scissors

Don't just carve jack-o'-lanterns this Halloween—make some edible ones, too! Using a basic cupcake recipe, you can create these funky cakes with pumpkin-orange frosting. A few marshmallows snipped into shape, and your grimacing cupcakes are ready to eat.

Step 1
Preheat the oven to 350°F (180°C).

Step 2
Line the muffin pan with the muffin cases.

Step 3
Put the butter and sugar into the mixing bowl and cream together with a wooden spoon until fluffy. If you wish, you can use an electric mixer for this step.

Step 4
Add the flour, baking powder, salt, eggs, vanilla extract, and milk. Use a wooden spoon or electric mixer to beat the ingredients together until the mixture is thick and smooth.

Step 5
Mix drops of orange food coloring into the cake batter until you have a pumpkin-like color.

Step 6
Spoon the mixture into the muffin cases, dividing it equally.

Step 7 Bake the cakes for 20–25 minutes. To test if the cakes are baked, insert a metal skewer into one cake. If it comes out clean, the cakes are ready.

Step 8 Place the cakes on a wire rack and allow to cool completely.

Step 9 To make the frosting, mix the powdered sugar, butter, and milk until it is thick and smooth. Put a couple of small spoonfuls into a separate dish.

Step 10 Add orange food coloring to the bigger quantity of frosting, and green coloring to the smaller quantity.

Step 11 To make one jack-o'-lantern, take two cakes and carefully slice off the rounded tops with a serrated knife.

Step 12

Spread orange frosting on top of one cake. Then turn the other cake upside down and put it on top of the frosting.

Green frosting

Icing syringe

Step 13

Using an icing syringe (or a spoon), add some green frosting to the top of the cake.

Use the black frosting to draw on eyes and a nose.

Step 14

Carefully cut triangular teeth from the marshmallows and press them into the frosting.

You can add some green sprinkles, too.

Enjoy!

Ingredients:

- 12 precooked sausages (or 24 cocktail sausages)
- 1 can of crescent roll dough (enough to make 6 rolls)
- 1 tablespoon honey
- 1 tablespoon ketchup
- 2 slices of any white cheese
- Mustard
- 3 black olives
- Cooking oil or spray for greasing

Equipment:

- Baking pan
- 2 brushes
- Small bowl
- Spoon
- Small sharp knife
- Oven mitt
- Potholder
- Scissors

Sausage Mummies

Have fun turning some ordinary sausages into these cool, spooky snacks. All you need to make the bandages for these delicious Halloween mummies is a tube of dough for crescent rolls. Let's get wrapping . . .

Step 1 Preheat the oven to 350°F (180°C).

Step 2 Brush or spray the baking pan with a little oil. This will keep your mummies from sticking to the pan.

Step 3 In a small bowl, mix the ketchup and honey together.

Step 4 Use the brush to cover the sausages in a light coating of the ketchup and honey mixture.

Step 5

Open the can of dough mix. Gently unroll the dough. A can with enough dough for six crescent rolls will contain three rectangles of dough.

Roll of dough

Rectangle of dough

Step 6

Take one rectangle, and with your fingers, squeeze together the diagonal **perforations** to make a smooth rectangle of dough.

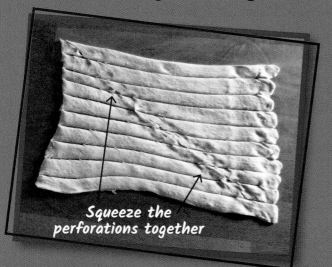

Squeeze the perforations together

Next, carefully cut the dough into strips. Each strip should be about half an inch (1 cm) wide.

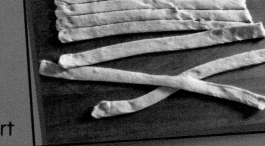

Step 7

Take one strip and start to wrap it around a sausage.

The ends of the strip will stick to the ketchup and honey mixture. Add a second strip of dough if needed. Leave an open space for the mummy's eyes.

Step 8 Place the mummies onto the baking pan and bake for 20 minutes. The mummies are ready when the dough bandages have turned a golden brown color.

Step 9 Using an oven mitt, carefully take the baking pan from the oven. Set the pan on a potholder to allow the mummies to cool.

Step 10 Cut tiny circles from the cheese slices and use a tiny blob of mustard to stick them to the mummies. Then cut tiny pieces of black olive (as pupils) and place one piece on each cheese circle.

Step 11 Your sausage mummies are ready to eat. Serve them drizzled with ketchup for a gory, bloody effect!

Cinnamon-Spiced Baked Apples

Ingredients:

- 4 Granny Smith or other cooking apples
- 4 tablespoons honey
- ½ teaspoon cinnamon
- 1 large orange
- 2 cups blackberries (fresh or frozen)

Equipment:

- Apple corer
- Knife and chopping board
- Small foil dish or shallow baking pan
- Grater
- Hand juicer
- Small dish
- Spoon
- Oven mitt
- Potholder

This next baked dish makes a great dessert for a chilly Halloween night. Sweet, spicy, and healthy, these baked apples with blackberries can be served with whipped cream or ice cream. You can even go apple picking yourself!

step 1
Preheat the oven to 350°F (180°C).

Cooking apple

Blackberries

step 2
Wash the apples and blackberries thoroughly. Wash the orange's skin, too.

step 3
Carefully core the apples, leaving a hole just a little bigger than a quarter.

Next, carefully make a cut around the center of each apple, just cutting through the skin.

step 4
Set the four apples in the foil dish or baking pan.

Step 5
Finely grate the orange's rind. Then cut the orange in half and squeeze out all its juice with a hand juicer.

Orange zest

Hand juicer

Honey

Cinnamon

Step 6
In a small dish, mix together the honey, cinnamon, and orange zest.

Step 7
Spoon an equal amount of the honey mixture into the hole in each apple. Pour the orange juice into the dish.

Step 8
Bake the apples for about 30 minutes. Remove the apples from the oven and set the dish on a potholder. Spoon the juices over the apples. Then spoon the blackberries over the apples, letting them spill into the dish. Return to the oven for about 15 minutes.

Step 9
Remove the apples from the oven and serve while hot.

The quantities on this page will make up to 16 portions

Ingredients

- 1½ cups of semisweet chocolate (broken into small pieces)
- 1 stick of butter or margarine
- 4 tablespoons of corn syrup
- 4 cups of Rice Krispies
- 1 cup mixed dried fruits
- 2 heaping cups of mini marshmallows
- 1 cup of white chocolate (broken into small pieces)
- Your choice of Halloween candy, including vampire teeth, severed fingers, snakes, gummy worms, and other gruesome, chewy treats

Equipment

- Rectangular baking pan approximately 12 inches × 8 inches (30 × 20 cm)
- Plastic wrap
- Large mixing bowl
- Wooden spoon
- 2 small saucepans
- Small bowl
- Chopping board and large knife

Squeamish Rubble

While the oven is full of delicious cupcakes and roasting mummies, get mixing and making this fantastic sweet party dessert. There's measuring, melting, and decorating to be done. So this recipe is perfect to make with friends!

Step 1
Line the baking pan with plastic wrap. Make sure the plastic wrap hangs over the edges of the pan.

Step 2
Add the Rice Krispies, dried fruit, and marshmallows to the mixing bowl.

Dried cranberries

Dried blueberries

Mini marshmallows

Rice Krispies

Syrup

Step 3
Add the semisweet chocolate, butter, and syrup to a saucepan.

Semisweet chocolate

Stick of butter

Step 4 Heat the saucepan on a medium heat. Stir the mixture until the chocolate and butter melts and all the ingredients are combined.

Step 5 Pour the melted chocolate mixture into the mixing bowl and gently stir until all the dry ingredients are coated with chocolate.

Step 6 Spoon the mixture into the baking pan and gently press it down.

Step 7 Melt the white chocolate pieces using the method described on page 9.

Step 8 Using a small spoon, drizzle the melted white chocolate over the mixture in the baking pan.

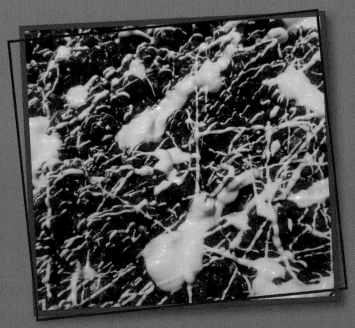

Step 9 Finally, decorate the rubble with Halloween candy and other gory treats. Gently press the candies onto the mixture.

Step 10 Place the pan of rubble mixture into the refrigerator to chill for at least an hour. (Alternatively, make this recipe the day before your Halloween celebrations.)

Step 11 When the rubble has set and is firm, gently lift the plastic wrap and slab of rubble from the pan and place on a cutting board.

Step 12 Carefully cut the rubble into chunks that measure about 2 inches by 2 inches (5 × 5 cm). Then heap the chunks of rubble on a plate and scatter with more candy!

Enjoy your squeamish Halloween rubble!

Glossary

beat

To blend a mixture of ingredients until they are smooth with equipment such as a spoon, fork, hand whisk, or electric mixer.

consistency

The thickness of a substance. For example, peanut butter has a thick consistency, while milk has a thin consistency.

cream together

To beat butter or margarine, usually with sugar, to make it light and fluffy.

dough

A thick mixture of flour, a liquid such as water or milk, and other ingredients, used for making baked goods such as bread and cookies.

drizzle

To trickle a thin stream of liquid (such as runny frosting or a sauce) over food.

glaze

A liquid that dries and gives an item, such as a cake or cookie, a shiny surface.

knead

To press, squeeze, and fold dough with your hands to make it smooth and stretchy.

perforations

A line of tiny holes or slots in a material that make it easier to tear the material along that line.

preheat

To turn on an oven so it is at the correct temperature for cooking a particular dish before the food is placed inside.

zest

The brightly colored outer part of the rind of citrus fruits, such as lemons and oranges.

Index

Further Information

Vanilli, Lily. *A Zombie Ate My Cupcake!: 25 Deliciously Weird Cupcake Recipes for Halloween and Other Spooky Occasions.* CICO Books, 2016.

Learn cool facts about Halloween here!
www.dkfindout.com/us/explore/11-spooky-facts-about-halloween/